AUTISM: Now What?

By Abby Ward Collins & Sibley J. Collins
Illustrated by Kimberly L. Owsley

This book donated by:

Autism Advocates of Indiana, Inc.
www.AutismIndiana.4T.com

With Funds raised at:

The 2001 "Answers for Autism" Walk

For more information about autism and autism resources in Indiana.

Indiana Resource Center for Autism
(812) 855-6508   http://www.iidc.indiana.edu/irca/

Phat Art 4
P.O. Box 711
Stratham, NH 03885-0711
Phone: (603) 778-9990
Fax: (603) 778-9669
publisher@phatart4.com

Visit our Website
www.phatart4.com

Toll-free Order Line
(866) 742-8278

First Edition, April 2002
ISBN #0-9706581-6-8

For our children
Kimberly, Stephany, Richard & Laura

Table of Contents

Who will benefit from this book?
My child has PDD-NOS, not autism. Will this
    book help me?
How can such a little book teach me all I need to
know about autism?

What tests will my child need?
Why is it sometimes difficult to get a diagnosis?
I wanted answers to my child's challenges…
    so why am I so angry?
Will I ever feel better about all of this?

What is Autism?
Autism: A Simplified Explanation for Parents
    and Children
Is autism genetic?
I hear people talking about "environmental
    factors." What does that mean?
Is it something I did?
I'd like to have another child. What are the
    chances of my second child having autism too?
How many people have autism?
Is there a cure?
Exploring Treatment Options

AUTISM: Now What?

Isn't that the first reaction we all have after our child's diagnosis finally sinks in? Then, after the shock and disbelief
wears off a bit, we are left to our own devices to plan for our
child's complicated medical and educational needs. Where
do we begin? Unfortunately, most of us don't have a clue.

Many of us will turn to our
child's doctor for help,
only to be further
confused with a copy of
the diagnostic criteria for
autism. Others will turn
to their child's teacher,
who may very well be
learning about autism
herself. Most will seek

> **"Prior to receiving my
> son's diagnosis the
> only exposure I had to
> autism was the movie
> Rainman and the
> occasional TV Movie of
> the week...."**
>
> Abby Collins

out books on autism only to be overwhelmed by medical
jargon, or momentarily uplifted by authors suggesting the
possibly of a cure. We find bits and pieces of the puzzle
over time, but have difficulty putting it all together because
we can't see the "big picture."

AUTISM: Now What? is a concise, down-to-earth
guidebook that helps parents make sense of it all. It
answers many commonly asked questions, while gently
guiding parents through the myriad of medical and
educational options, social services, therapies, etc.

In addition to teaching you "the facts," we have also included Abby Collins' personal story of raising her own son with
autism. We hope that in reading Abby's story you will: 1)
feel validated in your own struggles; 2) gain additional
insight into what you can expect; and 3) relate on a more
personal level to the information you read in this book.

We are proud to bring you this new resource and wish you
the very best as you begin your own autism journey.

> Abby & Sibley Collins, Authors
> Parents of a 14-year old son with autism

Introduction

Who will benefit from this book?

AUTISM: Now What? is designed to be a primer for parents of children recently diagnosed with autism and for friends and family members who want to help.

Readers of this book are likely to fall into one of four categories:

- parents of newly diagnosed children
- parents seeking answers to their child's developmental delays
- friends and family members
- educators who are new to autism

My child has PDD-NOS, not autism. Will this book help me?

"Autism Spectrum Disorder" is an umbrella term that includes several diagnoses falling under the category of autism. These include: autism, high-functioning autism (HFA), pervasive developmental disorder (PDD), pervasive developmental disorder-not otherwise specified (PDD-NOS), Asperger Syndrome (AS), Rett's Disorder, and Childhood Disintegrative Disorder. Parents of children with any of these diagnoses will find this book helpful, since they all involve the same basic neurological challenges—but to different degrees.

For simplicity's sake, the term "autism" will be used throughout the book, as will the pronoun "he" when referring to a child with autism.

For lack of better terms, children with autism are sometimes referred to as being either "higher functioning" or "lower functioning." Higher functioning generally refers to children with Asperger Syndrome, PDD-NOS, and HFA. Children who are higher functioning are verbal and are more likely to attend public schools and achieve some level of independence as adults. Children who are lower functioning are often non-verbal, exhibit more challenging behaviors, and may require self-contained (special needs-specific) school settings. For the purposes of this book, all other references to autism will assume the person falls somewhere in the middle of the functioning scale.

How can such a little book teach me all I need to know about autism?

Frankly, it can't—and that's not its intention. *AUTISM: Now What?* is designed to be a "quick read." It provides answers to parents' first important questions in an easy-to-read format that provides a solid understanding of autism basics.

Suggestions for further reading are found in Chapter 9.

CHAPTER 1

Getting a Diagnosis

What tests will my child need?

Autism is a neurological (brain) disorder that cannot be diagnosed with any single test. Typically, the diagnosing physician will conduct a battery of tests to rule out possible biological causes for the child's symptoms. When all medical tests are negative, autism can be diagnosed based on behavioral observations.

Medical testing typically includes:

- Physical Examination
- Blood Tests
- Urine Tests
- MRI (magnetic resonance imaging)
- EEG (electroencephlagraph)

Your diagnostician may also suggest that your child be evaluated by the following professionals:

- Speech Pathologist
- Occupational Therapist
- Physical Therapist
- Audiologist

You may be reluctant to subject your child to all of the suggested evaluations, since similar therapeutic testing will be conducted at your child's school. However, written evalua-  tions from experienced, *independent* therapists of your own choosing will not only provide a solid baseline from which to measure your child's progress, but will also give you leverage as you begin advocating for your child's medical and educational services.

Why is it sometimes difficult to get a diagnosis?

As we discussed earlier, autism is a "spectrum disorder," one that encompasses a wide-range of abilities and challenges. Autism is also a "developmental disorder," one that is often difficult to differentiate from other developmental disorders, particularly at a very young age.

For this reason, pediatricians who are not well-versed in autism are often reluctant or unable to make a diagnosis. In this case, concerned parents must be vigilant in seeking second opinions from pediatricians and specialists. If you are concerned that your child may have autism, but have not yet received a diagnosis, you may want to consult one or more of the following professionals:

- developmental pediatrician
- neurologist
- child psychologist/psychiatrist

Regardless of which professionals you choose, make sure they have extensive autism experience.

I wanted answers to my child's challenges...so why am I so angry?

Since you are reading this book, it is likely that you have already received a diagnosis of autism for your child, or perhaps suspect autism may be the answer to your child's unusual behaviors and speech delays. Whether or not you have received an official diagnosis, you are likely to be sad, scared, stressed, and/or angry. Try as you might to find some "silver lining" in this dark cloud, there are none. To put it bluntly, this stinks!

To add insult to injury, you may have been put through the "mill" (medical and/or education systems) while trying to find answers to your child's challenges. If you were lucky, you had experienced professionals in your corner from the start—ones who put you on the right track—with minimal effort required on your part. In general, the more difficult the process, the more confused and angry you are likely to feel.

Will I ever feel better about all of this?

Yes, but it takes time. After the initial flood of tears...after you read this book and many others...after you attend countless conferences...after you make friends with other parents of children with autism...after it all starts making some sense to you...that illusive silver lining will eventually start shining through!

CHAPTER 2

The Basics

What is Autism?

Autism is classified in the *Diagnostic and Statistical Manual of the Psychiatric Association of America, Volume IV* (the DSM-IV) as one of the "pervasive developmental disorders of the brain." It is not a disease, and it is not contagious. People with autism are often very healthy otherwise and, for some unknown reason, are usually very attractive in appearance. (It must be their good-looking parents!) Symptoms typically appear during the first three years of childhood and continue throughout life. Studies of people with autism have found abnormalities in several regions of the brain that suggest that autism results from a disruption of early fetal brain development.

If you look up autism in several places, you are likely to find definitions that vary widely. We have come to think of autism as: A disorder of the brain that causes impaired social interaction, problems with verbal and nonverbal communication, and unusual or severely limited activities and interests. These symptoms can vary in severity. In addition, people with autism often have abnormal responses to sounds, touch or other sensory stimulation.

Most people, even those with some experience in the field, can read the various definitions of autism and still not grasp what it really means. Over the years since our own son was diagnosed, we have had many occasions to explain autism to both adults and children. Through this experience we have developed the following simplified explanation of autism and its many challenges.

AUTISM: A Simplified Explanation
for Parents and Children

Autism is caused by a difference in the brain. Since you cannot see the brain of a child with autism, and most people with autism are healthy and good-looking otherwise, autism is often called "an invisible disability." You will only notice that a person with autism has special needs by observing differences in his behaviors, speech, and interests.

The brain receives messages through the five senses (touching, seeing, hearing, smelling, and tasting). The information received by the senses travels through the nervous system to the brain. The correct region of the brain processes the sensory input and then the brain tells the body what to do (i.e., if you touch something hot, the message of the burning pain will travel to your brain and your brain will tell you to quickly remove your hand).

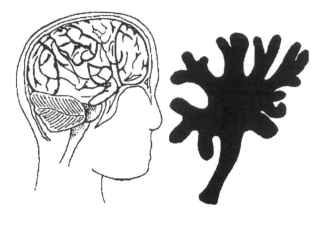

Brain   Dendrites (Brain Tree)

Everyone's brain contains a brain stem that receives the sensory information. The brain also contains dendrites, the neurons through which the sensory information travels. These dendrites look very much like the top of a tree, with a trunk (the brain stem), and many branches that reach out into the various sections of the brain. We call them "brain trees" (see figure above).

Everyone has a brain tree. The brain tree of a typical child will have many branches and from those branches, "twigs" that cover all the regions of the brain in just the right way. The branches are very healthy-looking, and there are a lot of them. The brain tree of a child with autism, however, is very different. Instead of strong, healthy limbs covered with twigs, the child with autism's brain tree will have fewer branches, and the branches they do have are likely to be frail and spindly-looking.

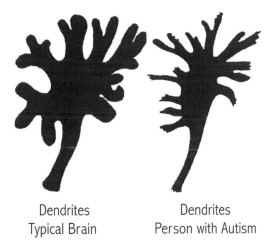

Dendrites
Typical Brain

Dendrites
Person with Autism

Each section of the brain manages certain aspects of the person's everyday functions. One section manages what the person sees. Other sections manage what he hears, his speech, balance, movements, thoughts, etc. When a typical child's brain receives sensory input, that information will go out to the proper branch of his brain tree and he will know exactly what to do.

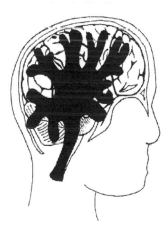

Brain of Typical Person

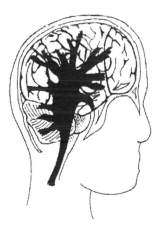

Brain of Person with Autism

8

However, sensory information entering the brain of a child with autism might not be able to reach its destination! What if the branch of the brain tree that processes what the child hears is cracked or broken? What do you think would happen inside the brain of a child with autism if his teacher said to him, "Johnny, please go to your desk, pick up a pen and bring it to me?" Johnny will hear the teacher (he is not deaf). He may even go to his desk to pick up the pen. However, some of the teacher's instructions are likely to get lost or confused in Johnny's brain. Would Johnny be able to do all of what the teacher asked? Probably not.

Think about the information we process through our sensory systems everyday. Those of us with more "typical" brains are, for the most part, able to figure out what to do and say at the proper time, have conversations with other people and understand things like competitive sports. We are also able to tune-out background noises, smells and other distractions as needed so that we can focus on what is important to us at any given moment.

Many people with autism also have what is known as sensory integration dysfunction. Since their brain trees are often lacking some of the limbs or twigs necessary to process all the input from their sensory systems, they often get anxious and frustrated. Many of the unusual behaviors exhibited by children with autism (self-stimming, spinning, rocking, self-injurious behaviors, lashing out at others, etc.) are simply attempts on their part to feel better in a world that must seem very confusing to them.

Does that mean we should let kids with autism do whatever they want?

Absolutely not. As members of society, they need to learn proper behaviors just like anyone else. They can, and do learn. They learn best in consistent, predictable environments where people understand their unique needs, are willing to learn about and make accommodations for their differences, have high expectations, respect for the child and a LOT of patience!

Is autism genetic?

Until recently, it was thought that autism was not genetic and occurred randomly in families. Recent studies, however, strongly suggest that some people do have a genetic predisposition to autism. Researchers are looking for clues about which genes contribute to this increased susceptibility. In some children, environmental factors also may play a role.

I hear people talking about "environmental factors." What does that mean?

Environmental factors relate to things that cause autism, or contribute to autistic-like symptoms after a child is born. Environmental causes include adverse reactions to vaccines, particularly the mercury that is used as a preservative. In some children the mercury may build up in their systems and alter brain development. Also, some children may develop autistic-like symptoms as a result of food allergies or yeast buildup (candida) in their systems.

Many environmental causes of autistic behaviors can be controlled with diet or through yeast or mercury reduction.

Environmental factors can also refer to a child's reaction to their surroundings, home life, parenting, etc. As recently as the 1960's, autism was often attributed to bad parenting, particularly on the part of the mothers. It was theorized that these cold, heartless "refrigerator mothers" were to blame for their children's autism. Thankfully, these theories have been disproven; after all, no one loves our kids more than we parents do!

Is it something I did?

No! But, you will undoubtedly wrack your brain trying to figure out what caused your child's autism. Mothers, in particular, often blame themselves. Was it that glass of wine you drank during your first trimester? Was it because your office was exterminated when you were pregnant?? Was it some karmic blunder that caused this dark cloud to descend upon you and your child??? The fact of the matter is, you will probably never know.

The only people who are fairly certain of a cause are parents whose children were clearly affected by a vaccine injury, or those whose children improve dramatically when given certain diet and therapeutic interventions. Most of us, however, simply have to learn to live with not knowing.

I'd like to have another child. What are the chances of my second child having autism too?

As we said above, there are genetic factors in autism, although no genetic markers have yet been clearly identified. Many people do go on to have additional children, and most of those children will be neuro-typical (or "tippies" as we like to call them—children who do not have developmental disabilities). There are no guarantees, however. Talk to your physician about your desire to have another child. Ultimately, though, you and your spouse/partner will have to weigh the potential risks for yourselves.

How many people have autism?

Autism statistics vary widely, depending upon which source you use. The Autism Society of America's statistics are currently at 1:500 (1 in every 500 babies born will have some form of autism); however, many highly respected medical professionals believe the ratio is closer to 1:250. Generally, the lower the ratio, the more likely it is that all forms of autism have been considered. Conversely, the higher ratio (1:1,000) is more accurate for the lower functioning (classic) forms of autism. Autism strikes males about four times more often than females.

Is there a cure?

There is no so-called "cure" for autism, and we would strongly caution anyone from spending vast amounts of money and countless hours in pursuit of one. Be especially wary of any program that guarantees a cure, or promises your child will enter first grade without an aide. As much as we all would like to think this is possible (and I'm not saying that miraculous improvements *never* happen!), common sense must dictate. Think about it. If these programs actually did offer a cure, wouldn't they be wildly famous? And, if there were a cure, wouldn't the incidence of autism be *decreasing*, rather than growing in record numbers?

If you are tempted to follow a program making fantastic claims, do your homework before signing on. Insist on talking with other families who have participated in the program. Realize they are likely to give you names of only satisfied customers, so you must ask some hard questions. What sacrifices (of time, money and family life) did they have to make to achieve results? Were the results long-lasting? Would they do it again?

Exploring Treatment Options

Parents may find these questions helpful as they consider various treatment programs:

- How successful has the program been for other children?
- How many children have gone on to placement in a regular school and how have they performed?
- Do staff members have training and experience in working with children and adolescents with autism?
- How are activities planned and organized?
- Are there predictable daily schedules and routines?
- How much individual attention will my child receive?
- How is progress measured? Will my child's behavior be closely observed and recorded?
- Will my child be given tasks and rewards that are personally motivating?
- Is the environment designed to minimize distractions?
- Will the program prepare me to continue the therapy at home?
- What is the cost, time commitment and location of the program?

What research is being done?

There are many studies aimed at identifying the causes and potential treatments/cure for autism. Some studies focus on the differences in the brains of people with autism. These tests are conducted using brain imaging and other innovative techniques. Other studies focus on identifying genes that increase the risk of autism and some evaluate infants, looking for the earliest signs of the disorder.

Researchers are also investigating how the brain develops and functions and how even small changes in brain structure and/or development can result in autism or autistic-like tendencies. Many of the newer studies are investigating vaccines, food allergies, and vitamin deficiencies as playing a role in the autism puzzle.

Researchers hope their work will provide new clues about how autism develops and how brain abnormalities affect behavior. To learn more about organizations conducting autism research, see Chapter 8.

CHAPTER 3

Medical and Therapeutic Options

What treatments are available?

There are many traditional and alternative treatments available. Therapeutic remedies help foster relatively normal development and reduce undesirable behaviors. Traditional therapies include:

- Speech & Language Therapy
- Occupational Therapy
- Sensory Integration Therapy
- Physical Therapy (not as commonly needed)

Every child with autism is likely to benefit from being evaluated and treated in these traditional areas. These treatments are usually available through school districts as part of the child's educational process, and through independent therapists. Your diagnosing physician will make recommendations about frequency and duration of therapy visits. Balance these recommendations against the very real limitations of your finances, insurance benefits, school cooperation and your own physical stamina in dealing with countless appointments! Try to find a balance that works not only for your child with autism, but for you, your family and your budget. This, of course, is not an easy task!

As with any therapy, results may take time. Try to be patient and celebrate every advance, no matter how small. In time, you are likely to see many improvements.

Will psychotherapy help?

Many parents of children with autism consult the services of psychiatrists, psychotherapists or other mental health counselors experienced in working with children with autism. The counselor will typically spend a portion of the session working

> "What people need to realize is that a major benefit of psychotherapy is the therapist *helping the parents learn to relate* to their child with autism."
>
> Teresa Bolick, Ph.D.
> Clinical Psychologist and Author of
> Asperger Syndrome & Adolescence

with the child at the child's own level and will then invite the parent(s) in to discuss his or her observations. Through these regular sessions, parents get a chance to ask questions and learn more about their child and what makes him tick. In addition, the counselor will often assist parents in coping with the impact of the autism on the marriage, siblings and extended family.

Will my child need to be medicated?

Not necessarily. Medications are often useful and appropriate in relieving many of the anxieties and compulsive-type disorders (symptoms) often associated with autism.

The decision to try prescription drug therapies is not one to be taken lightly. If your physician suggests medications and you are not comfortable with the recommendation, seek a second, and even a third opinion. Try to find a physician who is highly experienced with children who have autism. Further, it is always best to err on the side of caution and start with the smallest possible dose and increase only as needed.

My child's doctor doesn't think much of "alternative therapies," but I'm curious. Should I try them?

Physicians who are trained in traditional medical interventions will sometimes "poo-poo" the idea of alternative therapies. Being inexperienced in alternative treatments and concerned over the possibility of fleeting or inconsistent results, many conventional physicians dismiss the potential value of alternative therapies in favor of traditional therapies and/or pharmaceutical treatments.

This can be frustrating for parents. Parents are willing to try pretty much anything to help their child, preferring to start with options that have the greatest possible benefit with the least potential for harm. We look to our physicians to help us sort out ALL of the options, but it doesn't always work out that way. Sometimes parents must do some research and make these difficult decisions on their own.

Alternative Therapies

Alternative therapies provide additional options for parents anxious to reduce or eliminate some of the symptoms of autism. Results of these therapies will range from little change to drastic improvement to near-cure. Children with autism rarely have adverse reactions to alternative therapies, unless they are implemented carelessly or by unqualified people. It is important to remember that with healing methods that are non-pharmacological, their effectiveness is a complex mixture of technique, therapist, expectation and communication.

As with any intervention, parents need to do their homework and use common sense before implementing any new therapy. Also, very few alternative therapies are covered by insurance so parents must carefully pick and choose the ones that are most likely to be helpful.

What do I do when my child's professionals give me conflicting advice?

In addition to the myriad of therapeutic choices, parents will very often get conflicting advice from the professionals in their child's life. One caregiver will insist upon one treatment option, while a second opinion will yield a polar-opposite response. All we want is some sound advice but, more often than not, we leave these appointments more confused than ever! How can we...exhausted, emotionally compromised parents...be expected to "sift the gold" out of such a mixed pan of advice?

In fairness to professionals, that's what we pay them for. We *want* advice—we need to know what to do and how to do it. The difficulty comes in the implementation.

What sets us apart from the professionals, however, is the physical, emotional and spiritual attachments we have with our children... "parent's intuition," if you will. Think about it—how often have you been given what seemed like perfectly good advice, only to reject it because your "gut" told you something different? The specialists have years of experience and a host of degrees—but, let's face it, we have pretty smart guts! *Of course* we parents are the foremost experts! No amount of formal education can replace a parent's intuition, combined with good common sense. After all, we know our children and the dynamics of our families better than anyone.

This is not to suggest that we ignore or bypass professionals. Professionals have access to years of medical research, case histories, and what has worked best for other families. Their input helps us form the foundation of knowledge we need to access when making decisions for our children.

That's where intuition comes in. Take in all the advice you can get, combine it with your personal dreams and goals for your child and boil it down to gut instinct. Our "smart guts," however, will get us nowhere if we don't trust in them, and provide them with sufficient nourishment and exercise. You can accomplish this by:

- Continuing to learn as much as you can comfortably absorb about *all* children (not just your child with autism). It helps to know the typical developmental stages for all children so that we can aim toward, or even beyond, those goals.
- Accepting advice from everyone, making note of the similarities and differences in the advice.
- Seeking out counseling for yourself if you are confused, overwhelmed or feeling low.
- Taking a deep breath. Give yourself a pat on the back and a well-deserved break. You most likely do more in a day than many people accomplish in a week!
- Trusting in your ability to be a superb advocate— both as a loving parent and as the foremost authority on your child's needs.

CHAPTER 4

Special Education

Can my child be educated?

Yes. Even the most involved children with autism can (and do!) learn. Until just the last 20+ years, however, most people with autism were considered to be hopelessly mentally retarded. Many were home-schooled, if at all, and many more were institutionalized. Today, most children with autism are educated in inclusive (mainstreamed) public school programs or specialty programs designed to meet their unique needs.

**Early Supports & Services
(also called Early Intervention)**

As new parents plan for their child's education, most envision their youngster beginning school in either preschool or kindergarten. If your child's challenges (with or without a diagnosis) are identified prior to the age of three, however, it is likely his education will begin with Early Supports & Services (ES&S).

Early Supports & Services provides educational and therapeutic services to children ages 0-3. ES&S services are typically delivered through a combination of center-based therapies and playgroups and/or home visits. In addition, the caring professionals at your local ES&S center work with the *whole family* to help parents learn how to help their children…and themselves.

Transition to Public Preschool

Transitioning your child from the "warm & fuzzy" world of Early Supports & Services into the public preschool system can be a frightening time for parents. You will not be alone in the process, however. As the time of your child's third birthday draws near, ES&S professionals will begin assisting you with the transition process. The following questions and answers may also help put it in better perspective for you.

Answers to Parents' Most Frequently Asked Questions About Transition

1. *What happens when my child turns 3 and is no longer eligible for Early Supports & Services?* Children may participate in Early Supports & Services (ES&S) until they turn 3 years old. At that time they may be eligible to receive services through their public school. For those children who do go on to preschool special education at age 3, it is very important that everyone involved, the ES&S team, the parents and the public school start talking early...the earlier the better. Parents can start this conversation by calling the school district's special education department and asking to speak to someone about preschool special education. If a parent is uncomfortable making this first call, she or he may ask her ES&S team to contact the school district and refer her child.

2. *My child is turning three and I think he still needs help – what's next?* A team of professionals from your school district will gather information about your child through reports and evaluations to help determine whether there is a presence of an educational disability. This is a team decision and the parent is an important team member. If your child is determined to be eligible, an Individualized Education Plan (IEP) will be developed and a program will be determined.

3. *Is it possible that my child will not be eligible for preschool special education?* Yes. Eligibility criteria for Early Supports and Services are different than the criteria that school districts must use by law to determine eligibility for special education. It is possible that a child who received Early Supports & Services is not eligible to receive special education services.

4. *If my child is eligible, when will he start his preschool special education program?* The goal of a smooth and efficient transition is to complete all preliminary steps (information gathering, further evaluation if needed, determination of eligibility, IEP development and placement determination) just prior to your child's birthday so that everything is ready for him to start the new program when he turns 3.

5. *My child turns 3 in May...when will he begin his program?* If your child is eligible for special education services, when and where he will receive services is a team decision regardless of the time of year. Programming may begin in the summer if the team considers this necessary in order for him to receive educational benefits.

6. *What preschool placement options are available for my child?* According to federal and state laws, the child's "placement" is decided after his IEP is developed. Preschool placement options tend to vary from school district to school district; however, all are guided by the law's mandate that children be educated in the "least restrictive environment."

7. **Is my child required to attend an in-district preschool program?** This is an important question to discuss with the team after your child's IEP is developed. District policies do vary from town to town. Some towns that have few community programs may allow children to attend programs in "border towns." This is a decision to be discussed and determined by you and other team members.

8. **Can I visit and observe preschool programs before the placement decision is made?** Yes. Parents are encouraged to visit district preschool programs and/or community programs before final plans are made.

9. **My child is eligible for preschool special education but I don't think he's ready to attend a full program...can he receive just therapies?** Individual therapies cannot be provided in isolation, but rather must be related to your child's special education program. However, the program (including individual therapies) may be implemented in a variety of settings. The team will work with you to determine how your child's IEP goals can be appropriately implemented.

10. **Who pays for my child's preschool special education program?** The school district is financially responsible for providing an appropriate special education program that meets each child's individual needs as outlined in his IEP.

11. *Can my child attend preschool programming if he's still in diapers?* This is not a problem for school district preschool programs. However, some community (private) preschools and kindergartens do require that children be potty trained. This is an important topic for the team to discuss when determining the appropriate placement for your child.

12. *How will my child get to and from her preschool program?* Parents may choose to transport their child and take advantage of the daily informal opportunity to visit the classroom and "catch up" with teachers. If it is included in your child's IEP (as a related service), the school district will make arrangements (and pay) for transportation.

The preceding Q&A's were excerpted from the book "Change is in the Air: Transition...a Process of Anticipation, an Occasion for New Opportunities and Challenges," developed by the PTAN Region 5 Transition Work Group. Used with the permission of PTAN (Preschool Technical Assistance Network) and SERESC (Southern Regional Education Service Center), Bedford, NH.

Educational Program Options

There are many educational programming options available to children with autism. These include, but are by no means limited to:

- Inclusive education in your neighborhood schools
- Home-schooling (either on your own, or combined with home-based programs designed especially for children with autism)
- Applied Behavior Analysis (ABA) Programs (often a combination of school and home programming)
- Day schools for children with special needs
- Residential programs for children with special needs

There are many excellent publications covering a wide variety of education options for children with autism. See Chapter 9 for a listing of recommended books.

Public School

According to IDEA (the Individuals with Disabilities Education Act), every child with special needs is entitled to a "free and appropriate education in the least restrictive environment." If your child is determined by the school district to have special education needs, then your child will be eligible for the full-range of educational services mandated by the Federal Government. The services your child receives will be determined by the child's special education team as part of the development of the Individualized Education Plan (IEP).

As a parent of a child with autism you are an important member of the IEP team and are entitled to certain rights. By law, your school's special education director must give you a document outlining these rights at every IEP meeting.

Ensuring your child has appropriate educational and therapeutic services is not always easy. As stated above, parents are a very important part of a child's IEP team. As a team member, you will be able to participate fully in IEP meetings and offer recommendations as to what you believe to be appropriate services for your child. If you are lucky (and many parents are!) you and the rest of your child's team will see eye-to-eye on most issues and the process will go very smoothly. When this is the case, you will enjoy open dialogues with the team and everyone will look forward to the opportunity to get together and discuss your child's needs.

On the other hand, team members representing the school will not always agree with you. On occasion, they may not agree with your diagnosing physician either! These disagreements make for some tense moments, which only add to your difficulties as a parent of a child with autism. There are ways of dealing with these conflicts and they are described in the "Parent's Rights" forms you'll receive from your special education director.

Remembering to Give Thanks

Educators and therapists work hard, often at a level of pay that is not commensurate with their education. They made a *conscious choice* to work with our very challenging children and, in order to fulfill that goal, went to school for many years. There are times when they are stuck between a rock and a hard place—trying to do what's best for the children, while answering to administrators and their budgets.

Surely there will be days when you are frustrated with your child's professionals (and they with *you*!). Try to always remember, though, that their hearts are in the right place...and to be sure to thank them now and then!

IEP Meeting Tip: Bring a framed photo of your child to the next IEP meeting and place it in the middle of the conference table. Seeing your child's adorable, hopefully smiling, face will keep everyone mindful of you are all there!

CHAPTER 5

Advocating for Your Child's Needs

Advocate is a word you probably didn't use too often in your pre-autism vocabulary. *Merriam Webster's Collegiate Dictionary Tenth Edition* describes an advocate as "one who pleads the cause of another; to plead in favor of." As a parent of a child with autism, you will be doing a great deal of advocating…a great deal of *pleading*.

Advocacy generally starts in the medical arena with a parent's search for answers. Discontent to allow their child's developmental delays to go unchecked, parents begin the difficult process of having their child evaluated. Starting with their pediatricians, parents seek out the opinion of specialists and, perhaps for the first time in their lives, will come to question the opinion of medical professionals. Parents will also have to advocate for medical insurance coverage for some of their child's unusual medical needs.

Next comes educational advocacy. As a parent of a child with special educational needs you will be involved in every minute detail of your child's educational programming. At first parents may need to rely on the recommendations of the educational team but, with experience, will come to have strong opinions of their own regarding their child's educational needs.

You will also advocate for your child's social inclusion. It is often very difficult to include children with autism into typical social situations, so it'll be up to you to find ways to make it work for your child. Your local schools, area agencies, support groups and parent training centers are likely to have ideas for appropriate programs.

Advocating for your child can be both frustrating and tremendously rewarding. Be patient with yourself as you learn to "work the systems" to get your child what he needs.

Joining a support group is a great way to learn how to advocate. In addition to regular information and emotional support, you will also learn:

- what has worked for other parents
- what services are available
- when to apply for services (i.e., summer school)
- how to work with insurance companies
- if and when to hire a professional advocate

CHAPTER 6

Family Issues

An autism diagnosis affects not only the child and his parents, but also the siblings, grandparents and other extended family members. Parents are often so involved in their own fear and sorrow that they are sometimes unaware of the concerns of those closest to them.

Siblings have an especially difficult time. Older siblings, who may have resented the very birth of the child with autism, will further resent the extraordinary amount of care and attention that must be given this "intruder" following the diagnosis. Siblings, out of necessity on the part of the parents, are also dragged around to therapy appointments. Further, they observe their younger brother or sister "playing" with therapy equipment and wonder why they can't join in the fun. Try to spend some quality time alone with the sibling whenever possible, helping them to know how special they are too! Time alone with your more "typical" child will also help remind you of your life outside of autism. (You do have one, you know!)

Aunts and Uncles will show their concern in many different ways. Many will want to help, but won't know how. Some will try to minimize the parents' concerns, suggesting perhaps that the parents are making a big deal over nothing. Although these types of comments can be frustrating for parents, try to remember that most people really do mean well.

Grandparents have a particularly difficult time with the diagnosis in that they essentially mourn twice...once for the pain their own children are going through...and once for the loss they feel for their beloved grandchild's future. Grandparents also have the distinct disadvantage of having lived at a time when autism was essentially a taboo subject. People with autism were home-schooled or institutionalized, so little was known about it and few people spoke of it. Therefore, when grandparents hear the "A-word" they are much more likely to think the worst and may even be a little defensive. In their day, such a disability was a scourge of sorts on the family and, as such, some grandparents may be tempted to "assign blame" on the in-law's genes and/or the in-law's parenting skills.

Most grandparents will eventually, if not immediately, come to be the parents' greatest supporters. Once they learn about autism and its many forms, they will come to accept the reality of their grandchild's special needs and will want to help in any way they can.

CHAPTER 7

Helpful Hints & Coping Strategies

Communication

Every child needs some form of communication, whether or not they are able to speak. The sooner they are able to communicate, the less frustrated they will be. Even though speech is the goal, try not to resist therapists' and teachers' suggestions regarding sign language and visual communication systems. These alternatives often provide excellent "bridges" toward communication.

Your child may enjoy learning how to finger spell, using American Sign Language. In addition to learning a new skill, it's a fun way to help them reinforce the learning of new spelling words (by saying, writing *and* signing them)!

Even though your child may not speak, it is likely that he understands a lot more than you might think. Try to avoid talking in front of him, especially when relating your fears. Children with autism tend to be very intuitive.

Consistent Routine

Consistent routines will help your child feel more organized and reduce difficult behaviors. Try to establish routines around every day activities, i.e., bathroom and bedtime routines, meals, etc.

Difficult Situations

Keep an assortment of favorite toys and "surprises" handy to amuse your child in difficult situations (i.e., doctor's appointments).

Social situations are likely to be overwhelming for your child and will cause behavior problems like tantrumming or running away. Limit social exposure when absolutely necessary, but don't eliminate it altogether. Your child needs to learn to be part of the world.

Traveling and/or visiting relatives can be very stressful for people with autism. You may want to bring a blanket for the car ride (for comfort or to help avoid sun glare) and allow your child to find a safe, quiet place where he can escape the "adoring Aunties" and noisy cousins if needed.

When visiting a new place, allow your child to explore the new location (supervised, of course!). Fully exploring a new place, usually by walking the perimeter of a room or building, will create a sense of calm and make the visit more successful.

When strangers or family members criticize your child's behaviors (or YOUR lack of parenting skills), take advantage of the opportunity to teach them about autism and its many forms. This public service assumes, of course, that you aren't furious...or crying!

Eating Issues

If your child's food preferences are limited, try introducing new foods by dipping them into favorite sauces or condiments. Ranch dressing and ketchup are favorites.

Medical Appointments & Procedures

If at all possible, bring your child into the doctor's office for a visit a week or two *before* the actual appointment. Let him look around, meet the nurse, see where the bathroom is, etc.

☙ If your child needs to have a medical procedure requiring an IV or a blood draw, ask your physician to first apply an EMLA patch to the injection site. When applied one hour in advance, you child will not feel a thing! NOTE: EMLA patches are not helpful for deep muscle injections.

Parents' Needs

Assign the same level of importance to finding a great respite provider that you would in finding your child a good therapist. Your need for regular breaks is no less important than *anything* you do for your child!

Don't beat yourself up if you have neither the time, energy, nor the inclination to sit on the floor and work with your child for hours on end. You can only do what you can do!

Regressions

Your child is likely to have at least one or two regressions per year (spring and fall are common times). It's not uncommon for a child with autism to take "five steps forward and two steps back." Instead of dwelling on the temporary backslide, try keeping in mind that technically he has GAINED three steps!

School

When preparing for the first day of school, ask your child's teacher if you can bring your child in a few days in advance to visit his classroom and meet the teacher, aide and therapists. If at all possible, bring a video camera with you and videotape the child's entire experience— from getting out of the car at the school, until you leave. Be careful to make sure that you take him directly to his classroom, using the route that he will use daily (ask ahead of time to be sure). Allow your child to watch the video over and over before he starts school and you may be surprised how calm he is on the first day!

Sensory Challenges ₐ

Tags in clothing and seams in the toes of socks are often extremely irritating. Cut out the tags and, if possible, pre-wash all new clothing. If socks are a problem, seamless socks can be purchased through Sensory Comforts (see Chapter 8).

New shoes can also be a problem. If you find a pair of comfortable, easy-to-secure shoes (i.e., velcro), you may want to buy additional pairs of the same shoes in larger sizes.

Visual Aides

Children with autism are visual learners. Use visual aides whenever possible. A homemade "What Are We Going to Do Today?" chart, complete with velcro-backed photos or drawings will help organize the child's day. Similarly, a "Where Are We Going Today?" chart, hung from the back of the driver's seat car, is likely to reduce a child's anxiety about multiple stops in a car. Schools typically use these types of charts to visually organize schoolwork and activities.

Children with autism enjoy having their own calendar. They do a lot of calendar work at school and seem to appreciate a calendar's consistency (the same days, weeks, months...year after year!). Most children will enjoy crossing off each day at bedtime and will want to include special events on their calendars (birthdays, holidays, etc.). Colored stickers are a plus!

Social Stories introduce social situations to children. These simple "stories," written by the child's parents or teachers, typically include illustrations of some kind— ranging from stick figures to actual photographs. Social stories are an excellent way to prepare children with autism for new situations, or to help them work through challenging behaviors.

Maintaining a sense of humor will carry you through many a tough time. The following suggestions are fun ways to lighten up an otherwise difficult day!

How To Keep A Healthy Level Of Sanity

1. Sit in your parked car with sunglasses on and point a hair dryer at passing cars. See if they slow down.

2. Every time someone asks you to do something, ask if they want fries with that.

3. Finish all your sentences with "in accordance with the prophecy."

4. Ask people what sex they are. Laugh hysterically after they answer.

5. Specify that your drive-through order is "to go."

6. Go to a poetry recital; and ask why the poems don't rhyme.

7. Go to the opera and sing along with the cast.

8. Have friends and coworkers address you by your wrestling name, Rock Hard Kim/Ken.

9. Five days in advance, tell your friends you can't attend their party because you're not in the mood.

10. When the money comes out of the ATM, scream "I won! I won! Third time this week!"

CHAPTER 8

Resources

Autism National Committee (AUTCOM)
P.O. Box 6175
North Plymouth, MA 02362-6175
www.autcom.org/

Autism Research Institute (ARI)
4182 Adams Avenue
San Diego, CA 92116
www.autism.com/ari
Tel: 619-281-7165
Fax: 619-563-6840

Autism Society of America
7910 Woodmont Ave., Suite 300
Bethesda, MD 20814-3015
www.autism-society.org/
Tel: 301-657-0881 or 800-3-AUTISM (328-8476)
Fax: 301-657-0869

Center for Outreach and Services for the Autism
Community (COSAC)
1450 Parkside Avenue, Suite 22
Ewing, NJ 08638
www.njcosac.org/
Tel: 609-883-8100 or 800-4-AUTISM (428-8476)
Fax: 609-883-5509

Cure Autism Now (CAN) Foundation
5455 Wilshire Blvd., Suite 715
Los Angeles, CA 90036-4234
www.cureautismnow.org/
Tel: 323-549-0500
Fax: 323-549-0547

Families for Early Autism Treatment (FEAT)
P.O. Box 255722
Sacramento, CA 95895-5722
www.feat.org

National Alliance for Autism Research (NAAR)
99 Wall Street
Research Park
Princeton, NJ 08540
www.naar.org/
Tel: 609-430-9160 or 888-777-NAAR (6227)

National Autism Hotline
Autism Services Center
605 Ninth Street, Prichard Bldg.
Huntington, WV 25701-0507
Tel: 304-525-8014
Fax: 304-525-8026

MAAP Services (for Asperger's/High Functioning Autism)
P.O. Box 524
Crown Point, IN 46308
www.maapservices.org/index.html
Tel: 219-662-1311
Fax: 219-662-0638

Treatment and Education of Autistic and Related
Communications Handicapped Children (TEACCH)
The University of North Carolina
310 Medical School – Wing E
Chapel Hill, NC 27599-7180
Tel: 919-966-2174

Online Support

Autism Resources
www.unc.edu/~cory/autism-info/

Online Asperger Syndrome Information & Support (OASIS)
www.udel.edu/bkirby/asperger/

PDD Support Home Page
www.thelaughtongroup.com/pddsupport/index.html

Online Education

WebED, Inc. provides a wide variety of on-line continuing
education courses for teachers and paraprofessionals.

WebED's courses on autism are available free to parents.
Visit www.WebED.com and go to the Parents' Autism Catalog
for instructions on accessing these courses.

Online Autism Products

BrainChild Nutritionals
Offers natural nutritional support products for people with autism spectrum and attention deficit disorders.
www.brainchildnutritionals.com

Gluten-Free Pantry
The Gluten-Free Pantry offers a wide variety of gluten and casein-free food products and recipes.
www.glutenfree.com

Phat Art 4
A publishing company dedicated to producing and distributing down to earth books on autism and related disorders. Over 150 titles.
www.phatart4.com

Sensory Comfort
A mail order company dedicated to "Making Life More Comfortable for Children and Adults who have Sensory Processing Differences."
www.sensorycomfort.com

Southpaw Enterprises
Offers a variety of occupational therapy products including: weighted blankets and vests, suspended equipment, therapy balls, etc.
www.southpawenterprises.com

CHAPTER 9

Recommended Reading

The following are just a few of the excellent books available to anyone who is new to the autism field.

Parent/Family Guides

Children with Autism II: A Parents' Guide
  by Michael D. Powers, Psy.D.
If you've ever wanted to crawl in the closet with an OREO...
  by Martha Kate Downey
From the Heart – Edited by Jayne D.B. Marsh
Let Me Hear Your Voice by Katherine Maurice
Negotiating the Special Education Maze by Winifred Anderson,
  Stephen Chitwood & Deidre Hayden
**Right from the Start: Behavioral Intervention for Young Children
    with Autism** by Sandra L. Harris Ph.D., Mary Jane Weiss, Ph.D.
Uncommon Fathers – Edited by Donald J. Meyer

Sibling Books

Autism Through a Sister's Eyes by Eve B. Band & Emily Hecht
I Love My Brother! by Connor Sullivan
Siblings of Children with Autism by Sandra L. Harris, Ph.D.
Views from Our Shoes – Edited by Donald J. Meyer

Children's Books on Autism

Captain Tommy by Abby Ward Messner
Tobin Learns to Make Friends by Diane Murrell
Trevor Trevor by Dr. Diane Twachtman-Cullen

Books Written by People with Autism

Beyond the Wall by Stephen Shore
Emergence: Labeled Autistic by Temple Grandin
Thinking in Pictures and Other Reports from My Life with Autism by Temple Grandin
Your Life is Not a Label by Jerry Newport

Asperger Syndrome

Asperger Syndrome by Tony Attwood
Asperger Syndrome & Adolescence
   by Teresa Bolick, Ph.D.
Asperger Syndrome & Difficult Moments
   by Brenda Smith Myles and Jack Southwick
Asperger Syndrome & Sensory Issues by Brenda Smith Myles
Asperger Syndrome in the Family
   by Liane Holliday Willey
Pretending to be Normal by Liane Holliday Willey

Children's Books on Asperger Syndrome

Asperger Syndrome, the Universe & Everything by Kenneth Hall
Asperger's: What Does it Mean to Me? by Catherine Faherty
Tap Dancing in the Night by Martha Kate Downey

Teacher Resources

Activity Schedules for Children with Autism
   by Lynn E. McClannahan, Ph.D. & Patricia J. Krantz, Ph.D.
Do-Watch-Listen-Say by Kathleen Ann Quill, Ed.D.
How to be a ParaPro by Dr. Diane Twachtman-Cullen
Inclusive Programming for Elementary Students with Autism
   by Sheila Wagner

Books on Specific Topics

IEP Development

Creating a Win-Win IEP by Beth Fouse and Veronica Zysk, Editor
How Does Your IEP Measure Up? by Dr. Diane Twachtman-Cullen
and Jennifer Twachtman-Reilly

Medications

Taking the Mystery Out of Medications in Autism by Dr. Luke Tsai

Sensory Integration

Teachers Ask About Sensory Integration by Carol Stock Kranowitz
Unlocking the Mysteries of Sensory Dysfunction
by Elizabeth Anderson and Pauline Emmons

Sleep Challenges

Sleep Better! by V. Mark Durand, Ph.D.

Social Skills

Navigating the Social World by Jeanette McAffee, M.D.
Reaching out, Joining In by Mary Jane Weiss and Sandra L. Harris

Toileting

Toilet Training for Individuals with Autism and Related Disorders
by Maria Wheeler

Treatments, Diets & Alternative Therapies

Autism Treatment Guide by Elizabeth Gerlach
**Biological Treatments for Autism and PDD: What's Going On?
What Can You Do About It?** by Dr. William Shaw
Special Diets for Special Kids I & II by Lisa Lewis, Ph.D.
**Unraveling the Mystery of Autism and Pervasive Developmental
Disorder: A Mother's Story of Research and Recovery**
by Karyn Seroussi

Visual Aids

Activity Schedules for Children with Autism
by Lynn E. McClannahan and Patricia J. Krantz
Comic Strip Conversations by Carol Gray
The New Social Stories Book by Carol Gray

These books and many others can be obtained through
Phat Art 4 Publishing at www.phatart4.com
or call toll-free (866) 742-8278 to request a catalog.

CHAPTER 10

The Future

What does my child's future hold?

As we said previously, people with autism are typically very healthy otherwise and have normal life expectancies. How your child will fare in his teenage and adult years will depend on many factors. These include: 1) Where the child falls on the autism spectrum (higher or lower functioning); 2) educational and therapeutic interventions received; 3) at what age interventions began; 4) whether or not the child has other special needs in addition to the autism; and 5) if he has supportive family and friends.

Some people with autism grow up to live fairly typical lives; they live independently, drive a car, hold a job and share their lives with someone special. Most adults, however, require some level of support throughout their lives. The level of support needed depends upon the functioning level of the individual as he reaches adulthood.

GLOSSARY & ACRONYMS

AAC - Assistive Augmentative Communication

A speech-language therapist's term for communication using a picture board or recorded messages activated by buttons, etc.

ABA - Applied Behavior Analysis

Behavioral techniques that refer to a kind of careful analysis and tracking of behavior including its cues and consequences.

ABR - Auditory Brain Response

Refer to Auditory Evoked Response (AER)

ADA - Americans with Disabilities Act

USA law that ensures rights of persons with disabilities with regard to employment and other issues.

Adaptive Behavior

The ability to adjust to new situations and to apply familiar or new skills to those situations.

AER - Auditory Evoked Response
A test measuring the conductivity of the auditory nerve to the brain. (Does not require responses from the child.)

AIT - Auditory Integration Training

An alternative therapy method of reducing hypersensitivity to sounds at various frequencies.

Aphasia

Loss of ability to use or understand words.

Apraxia

The loss of ability to perform voluntary movements (i.e., the brain is unable to translate thoughts about moving into actual movement).

AS - Asperger's Syndrome

A pervasive developmental disorder characterized by significant impairment of social interaction and stereotyped patterns of behavior.

ASA - Autism Society of America

Augmentative Communication

Any method of communicating that utilizes an assistive technique or device such as signs, gestures, picture boards, etc.

Autistic Savant

An autistic individual who displays incredible aptitude in a particular skill.

Autistic Spectrum Disorders

Term that encompasses autism and related disorders.

Aversives

Behavioral methods employing punishment rather than positive reinforcement. Often involves physical pain.

Behavior Modification

A method of controlling behavior through the use of rewards and consequences.

Behavioralist

A person who observes behavior and then helps the child develop more adaptive alternative behaviors.

CDC - Center for Disease Control

Cognition

Thinking skills that include the ability to receive, process, analyze and understand information.

DD - Developmental Disabilities

A disabling condition that affects intellectual, functional and academic development from birth to age 22.

DTT - Discrete Trial Training

Sometimes referred to as Discrete Trial Therapy and Discrete Trial Teaching. The term is also often used in a less specific way, as a synonym for ABA.

DSM-IV - Diagnostic and Statistical Manual–4th Edition

Dyspraxia

A problem with praxis, i.e., planning, initiating, sequencing and carrying out volitional movements

Echolalia

Repeating back something said to you. Delayed echolalia is repeating it later. Both behaviors are found in many people with autism.

EEG - Electroencephalogram

A test consisting of recording brainwaves as picked up by electrodes. It is used to identify seizures.

Expressive Language

The ability to communicate thoughts and feelings through gestures, sign language, written word or verbalizations.

FC or F/C - Facilitated Communication

A technique that allows non-verbal people to communicate by typing on a computer keyboard, assisted by a person called a facilitator.

Fine Motor Skills

The developmental area involving skills that require the coordination of the small muscles of the body, including those of the hands and face.

Fragile X Syndrome

A genetic disorder named for the appearance of a broken or "fragile" X chromosome when exposed to certain chemicals in a laboratory setting.

Genetics

The study of conditions resulting from inherited components of DNA.

Gluten-Free/Casein Free Diet

An eating plan that removes gluten (wheat protein) and casein (milk protein) from a person's diet.

Gross Motor Skills

The developmental area involving skills that require the coordination of the large muscles of the body, including the legs.

HFA High-Functioning Autism

Hyperlexia/Hyperlexic

Ability to read at an early age, but often without linking the words to what they words mean.

Hypersensitivity

Over-sensitivity to sensory input (often to the point of pain).

Hyposensitivity

Under-sensitivity to sensory input, resulting in little or no response to noise, hot/cold, etc.

Hypotonia

Low muscle tone.

IDEA - Individuals with Disabilities Act

A US Law mandating a Free and Public Education for all persons with disabilities between the ages of 3 and 21.

IEP - Individualized Educational Plan

An individualized education program designed by a team comprised of the child's parents, regular education teachers, special education teachers, therapists, etc. This plan is designed to meet the individual needs of a child with educational disabilities.

IFSP - Individualized Family Service Plan

An individualized plan designed to meet the needs of children ages 0-3 and their families in Early Supports & Services/Early Intervention settings.

Inclusion or Mainstreaming

Placement of a disabled child with non-disabled peers in a regular classroom.

Ketogenic Diet

Restricted diet used to prevent epileptic seizures.

LD - Learning Disabled

LKS - Landau-Kleffner Syndrome

A seizure disorder that often has characteristics similar to autism.

Lovaas Method

An intensive behavior modification program created by Dr. Ivar Lovaas.

MRI - Magnetic Resonance Imaging

A diagnostic tool in the sense of an X-ray machine or CAT scanner which, like them, creates internal images of selected parts of the body. Rather than sending X-rays through the body, it builds its image data by testing the magnetism of the body tissue.

Naturopathy

Stanley Greenspan's term for an autistic-like set of symptoms.

Neuroleptic

A class of drug that includes Haldol and Risperdal.

Neurologist

A physician who specializes in disorders of the brain.

Neurotransmitter

A chemical substance found between nerve cells in the brain that allows sensory information/impulses to travel from one part of the brain to another.

NICHCY - National Information Center for Children and Youth with Disabilities

NIH - National Institutes of Health

NIMH - National Institutes for Mental Health

NT - Neurologically typical/neuro-typical

In conversations about autism, this term is often used to describe people who do not have an autism spectrum disorder.

OCD - Obsessive Compulsive Disorder

Oral Motor

Relating to the muscles of the mouth.

OT - Occupational Therapy or Occupational Therapist

A therapist specializing in improving the development of fine motor, gross motor and adaptive skills.

PDD - Pervasive Development Disorder

PDD-NOS - Pervasive Development Disorder—Not Otherwise Specified

PECS - Picture Exchange Communication System

An alternative communication system that uses picture cards.

PEP - Psycho-educational profile

A test designed to assess the presence of autism and point toward treatment strategies and some areas of need.

Perseveration

Obsessive-like repetition of a behavior.

Pragmatics

The understanding of how and why language is used—especially in social situations.

Proprioception

The body's conscious or unconscious awareness of its position in relation to its surroundings.

PT - Physical Therapy

Therapeutic treatment designed to prevent or alleviate movement dysfunction through a program tailored to the individual child. The goal of this therapy may be to develop strength, range of motion, coordination, etc.

Receptive Language

The ability to understand spoken and written communication, hand gestures and body language.

Related Services

Additional services at school that would help a child further benefit from his special education. These services might include speech, occupational therapy, transportation, etc.

Respite/Respite Care

Skilled, adult supervision of a person with special needs with the goal of giving the primary caregiver a break.

Savant

See Autistic Savant.

Secretin

A hormone used to diagnose digestive problems that is also helpful in reducing the symptoms of autism.

Self-Stimming, Self Regulatory and Self Stimulatory Behavior

Behaviors whose purpose appears to be to stimulate one's own senses (these include rocking and flapping).

Sensory Integration Therapy (SI)

A therapy that uses physical activities to help regulate the effect of and responses to sensory input.

Seratonin

A neurotransmitter (brain chemical) that plays a part in communication within the nervous system.

SLP - Speech-Language Pathologist

A therapist who works to improve speech/language and oral-motor skills.

Tactile

Relating to the sense of touch.

Vestibular

Sensory system located in the inner ear that allows the body to maintain balance.

A Family's Journey into Autism
by Abby Collins

Introduction

When my son was first diagnosed with PDD at the age of 3 1/2, I was most interested in learning "the facts" about autism and in reading other families' stories (I felt comforted in knowing others had lived to tell about it!). *AUTISM: Now What?* combines these two elements to bring you a primer on autism that is informative, insightful and validating to parents. I hope you enjoy my story.

This is a story about autism as seen through the eyes of a parent who has "been there." Through the telling of my family's story, I will provide a framework for some of the typical steps leading up to an autism diagnosis. Drawing from my own personal experience, I will illustrate how to identify some of the earliest signs of the disorder, the challenge of getting an accurate diagnosis, and the emotional roller coaster parents ride before, during and after hearing the dreaded words "your child has autism."

Before we begin, I would like to say that despite the many challenges autism imposes, it also offers a tremendous opportunity for personal growth. Much to my surprise, I have come to see it as something of a blessing. As a parent, would I want to rid my son of his autism if I could? In a heartbeat! But, even if that were possible, I would not want to rid myself of the memory of the experience. Because of the autism, I have grown in ways I never thought possible. I am much more sensitive to the needs of others. I take very little for granted, and can find delight in the strangest things. For example, instead of being devastated the first time my son said, "I hate you Momma!" I excused myself from the room, grinned from ear-to-ear, and jumped up and down, arms flailing, thinking "Wow! Two pronouns in one sentence!"

Throughout this journey I will be sharing some lighthearted moments and, whenever possible, pointing out what I have come to see as "bright sides." I do this not to make light of difficult situations, but to benefit the reader by reminding him or her of the upsides of this otherwise devastating disorder. Remember as you read, that my son's functional abilities fall in the middle of the autism spectrum, and much of what I will offer you will be from that perspective. I sincerely hope that every parent of a child with autism, or other developmental disability, will find useful information, validation and even some humor within these pages.

Roadblock: Infertility

From as far back as first grade, I never really knew what I wanted to be when I grew up. I always envied the certainty of my friends when they said, "I'm going to be a teacher," or "I'm going to be a nurse." All I knew was that I wanted to be a "mommy," and that any other potential career was secondary. So, you can imagine my dismay when infertility delayed my dream.

After months of temperature taking and invasive procedures, my doctors determined that my ovaries needed a chemical boost and prescribed a drug to help me conceive. I remember being very excited at the time—thinking we had found the answer to our problems. My husband wasn't so sure: "Do you know the statistics on this drug? Could we end up having twins or triplets—or more? Does this drug increase our changes of having a disabled child?" I dismissed my husband's concerns, assuring him that we would have the baby or babies that we were meant to have, and if they had special needs we would love them all the more. He very reluctantly agreed.

As it turned out, I had an adverse reaction to the prescribed drug. During the first five days of pills, I experienced every bad side effect noted on the drug information sheet. The hot flashes and visual distubances were unbearable and, according to my fertility specialist, the drug nearly ruptured my ovaries. Despite the discomfort, I continued on—only to face the disappointment of a negative pregnancy test result.

My doctors suggested I take a couple of months off to allow my ovaries to settle down, and then discuss alternative treatments. I remember going back to the doctor's office two months later—the day before Thanksgiving, 1986. In her office, the doctor said "Abby, I'm not sure what we can do for you." The initial treatment was the most gentle of all of the fertility drugs. My strong

63

adverse reaction to it had her concerned. She wanted to consult her colleagues in New York to see if they had any suggestions for my case. In the meantime, she wanted to re-induce my periods with drugs, but first had to rule out pregnancy.

I remember thinking how absurd it was to "rule out" pregnancy when that was the goal! As I handed the specimen cup to the nurse she asked cheerfully, "Would you like to wait for the results?" Obviously, she didn't know what had just gone on in her boss's office. "No, I don't want to wait," I said quietly, choking back tears. On my way back to work, I tried to pull myself together. I resented having to return to the office. It was Thanksgiving Eve, and the rest of the support staff was allowed to leave early. I returned to my desk, only to have my boss immediately start making demands. "Can't he see I've been crying?" I grumbled silently, wondering how anyone could possibly be so insensitive.

When the phone rang I did not recognize the voice that said slowly, almost teasing, "You should have waited!" After a few seconds I realized it was my doctor's nurse, and I asked nervously, "What do you mean?" "Your test was *positive*!" she replied excitedly. I all but called her a liar. "Don't do this to me!" I yelled into the phone, crying, thinking it was some incredibly cruel joke. She assured me there was no mistake. I sat there stunned, still wiping my eyes.

Knowing that he must have overheard my telephone conversation, I went into my boss's office. "I suppose you're wondering what that was all about?" Never one to want to know "too many details" he replied nervously, "Well, I could tell it was personal, so I was trying not to listen." I told him the whole story and he sat behind his big desk beaming, sharing in my delight. Needless to say, he finally let me go home!

All Packed and Ready to Go—To the Hospital, That Is!—Birth through 18 Months

Richard, my miracle baby, was 7 lbs., 8oz. and 20 inches long at birth—the size and weight the baby books considered "exactly average."

Home from the Hospital!

Richard was an incredibly good baby. He was sleeping through the night by the time he was four weeks old, and would take two well-spaced naps during the day. He rarely cried without an obvious reason for doing so. I could take him anywhere and he would lie there cooing, smiling and charming the socks off of anyone who would offer some attention. I remember one of my friends saying, "Oh, you'll never get another one as perfect as he is! You're soooo lucky!"

To the untrained eye, Richard did seem perfect. Even as he began walking (a bit late at fifteen months), he was still happy and engaging. He enjoyed the company of other children and was extremely affectionate. I have since learned some of the early signs of autism, many of which Richard exhibited, so I have little doubt that he was born with the disorder.

Signs of autism that I missed, include:

- Difficulty nursing.
- A fascination with overhead lights and ceiling fans.
- Playing with only parts of toys (i.e., a single wheel of a truck).
- Lining up objects in meticulous rows.
- Not wanting to open gifts.
- Walking around the perimeter of rooms, hugging the walls, while other children played.
- Locking himself in our bathroom, sitting happily alone in total darkness.
- Quietly crawling away—preferring to be alone.

- Screaming when we washed his hair or clipped his nails.
- Inability to tolerate tags in clothing, certain fabrics, new shoes.
- Flapping his arms, spinning himself around.
- Unusual food preferences (addicted to cranberry sauce).
- Undisturbed when a balloon popped loudly behind him (I thought he was deaf).
- Lying flat on the floor with his cheek pressed firmly against the cool marble flooring.

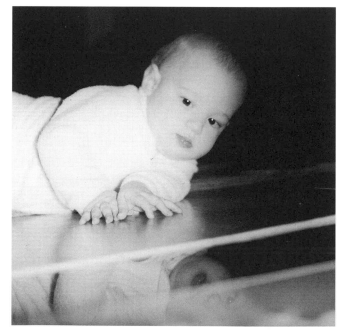

Richard at 9 months – His face reflected in the marble flooring he loved!

The First of Many Denials: 18–36 Months

My son's pediatrician exhibited concern when, at eighteen-months old, Richard was able to say only four or five words. I wasn't worried at the time, having been assured by family and friends: "He's your first born, and a boy no less—he'll talk when he's ready. Maybe *you* should stop talking for him!" With that somewhat obnoxious bit of denial firmly in my pocket, I told the pediatrician that I wasn't overly concerned, and asked if we could just take a "wait and see" attitude. He agreed, but insisted that I have Richard evaluated if he was still not talking at his twenty-four month checkup.

One reason for my resistance in taking action at that time was that I was four months pregnant with my daughter, Laura (another miracle!), and was physically exhausted. Fortunately, Richard napped a great deal. I took advantage of his schedule and napped right along with him. During my deepest periods of denial, I convinced myself that Richard's speech and language delays resulted from my being tired and not giving him enough attention.

Richard's speech and language had not improved by his twenty-four month checkup; instead, he had lost the few words he had been able to say, and was quickly retreating into his own little world. Richard's father and I began to worry somewhat at this point, but still hoped for the best as we prepared for Laura's arrival. Laura was born on December 29, 1989, and we brought her home on New Year's eve. I felt very much alone with the children at this point, as their father went back to work immediately and began putting in longer and longer hours. I gave him a lot of credit at the time, for working so hard to provide for his family, but I also suspected that at least part of his professional drive was fueled by a need to escape our growing concerns about Richard. I remember being jealous of that luxury.

In addition to the lack of support at home, my thrill over having a baby girl was also dampened by Richard's reaction to his baby sister. Unfortunately, Laura was not nearly as placid as as her brother had been and demanded a great deal of attention. As I tried to soothe her, Richard would sit in the far corner of the room and watch. He looked devastated, abandoned, and my heart broke every time I looked into his sad eyes. About a week later, however, I was sitting on the floor trying to get him to play ball with me. He looked at the ball, then at me, then took a long look at Laura's bassinet where she was sleeping soundly. Richard suddenly looked satisfied, as if he had realized that having a sister wasn't such a bad thing after all. He rolled the ball back to me with a smile.

Looking back at photos of Richard during that period, I cried when I noticed for the first time the abrupt shift he had made from a happy, engaged toddler to a sad, lost little boy.

Heeding the pediatrician's advice, but still certain deep down that he would get past this little setback, I took Richard to our local early intervention center to be evaluated. The folks at the Richie McFarland Children's

Center were tremendously supportive, both of Richard and our family. After evaluating his needs, they enrolled Richard in two toddler playgroups per week at the center. In addition, an early childhood educator came to our house once a week to work with Richard.

Through a two-way mirror, I would often observe Richard in his toddler groups. Unlike his group-mates, Richard did not exhibit any physical signs of disability, yet he wouldn't participate with the other children unless literally forced to do so. While the other children sat in a circle singing or blowing bubbles, Richard would walk around the perimeter of the room, desperately trying to find a door to escape through. After several weeks in the group, Richard relaxed a bit and participated more often.

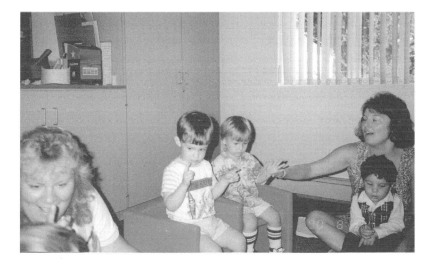

Richard learning sign language at the Richie McFarland Children's Center

Nonverbal at the time, his teacher taught him some simple communication signs using his hands (concepts such as *more*, *help*, *eat*, and *play*). At first, I balked at the idea of Richard signing, arguing that he was not deaf and that I wanted him to talk, not to sign. But I was wrong. Being able to communicate just those four basic concepts immediately reduced Richard's negative behaviors (mostly screaming) and quickly set the stage for more advanced communication.

At this time I still did not know Richard had autism. I learned a great deal, however, while observing the loving professionals as they worked with my son. Each of Richard's teachers and therapists took the time to teach me techniques that would help him grow.

I sat in on speech and occupational therapy sessions at least once a month. Each time I walked away with new ways of helping Richard cope in a world that was clearly overwhelming to him. I did not sit in on every session. Richard needed time to acclimate to the new people in his life and, just as important, I needed a break. Laura was a baby at the time. When I would take Richard for therapy, I would quite often leave her with a friend or baby-sitter. With Laura well cared for and Richard in the therapist's office, I would often retreat to somewhere quiet and read a magazine or just sit there, lost in my thoughts. This was *my* time. I had fifty precious minutes of respite, twice a week. I recommend that all parents carve out this kind of break for themselves, to recharge and regroup. Raising a child with autism is more of a marathon than a sprint! So pace yourself.

Aren't Play Groups Supposed to Be FUN?

In addition to having difficulty participating in the toddler groups at the early intervention center, Richard was also withdrawing from children he had known in play groups since he was about fifteen months old. These play groups were something of a lifeline for me, as they afforded me the opportunity to socialize with the other children's mothers as the children played together. As Richard's behavior grew more distant and downright bizarre, however, the groups were anything *but* fun. While the other children played with trucks and dolls, Richard would stand at the doorways, flicking lights on and off endlessly. On the occasions when he would play with what I considered to be "real toys," he would line them up in neat little rows and scream if one of the other children touched them or, heaven forbid, knocked them over.

The other moms in the play groups were sympathetic and I felt very supported during this time, even though we all felt powerless as we watched Richard go deeper and deeper into his own world. One day was particularly troubling. The playgroup met in the function room of a local church. On this particular day, there were about eight of us moms and about eighteen children between us. The other mothers and I sat and talked, glancing over occasionally to make sure the kids were all right. At one point, I couldn't spot Richard anywhere in the room. Sensing my alarm, the adults all stood up and started looking around. A minute or so later one of my friends called out, saying she had found Richard. There he was, sitting cross-legged in a corner behind a couple of room dividers. He had wiggled himself tightly into the corner and was staring at the wall. Some of the other children followed us over and the older ones tried to coax him out. He just sat—and stared.

I picked Richard up, still cross-legged, and took him and baby Laura home. He seemed to breathe a sigh of relief as I secured him into his car seat and he promptly fell asleep. I cried all the way home, knowing that I would soon have to give up the parent support/toddler play groups that had sustained me. My optimism about Richard overcoming what I thought were simple "speech issues" was beginning to wane. I can't recall my full range of feelings at the time, only that I felt a profound sense of dread.

Paddling Furiously Upstream in the River of Denial

When did I let down my guard and accept that we were in it for the long haul? Was it watching Richard walk around the room hugging the walls at the early intervention center while the other children played happily in groups? Was it the day I found him sitting alone, perfectly content in total darkness on our bathroom floor, the door shut behind him? No, what shook me violently into the reality of Richard's autism was his third birthday party at McDonald's.

This McDonald's had an indoor Playland. On this particular day, Richard was so overwhelmed by his party and all of the children buzzing around him that he simply shut down. He was sitting, almost catatonic, on the stairs

leading up to the slide that he absolutely loved.
The children, nearly all of them his invited guests, climbed over and around him, laughing and having a ball. Richard just sat there with a blank look on his face, seemingly oblivious to his environment. I suddenly realized I had seen that look on a TV "Movie of the Week" on autism. It felt like all of the blood was rushing from my body. I thought, "Oh man, it can't be . . . ."

Richard - Overwhelmed at his 3rd Birthday Party.

After hyperventilating in the rest room, I returned to the party to find that Richard had finally climbed the stairs, slid down and joined the others at the table. *Whew!* However, my concerns about what I now call his "autistic stare" were validated a week or two later, when his early childhood educator observed similar behavior on one of

74

her home visits. When she asked, "Have you seen him do this before?" with a very concerned look on her face, I knew my concerns were justified.

During this period I put many of Richard's educational and medical professionals on the spot by asking, "What do you think is wrong with him?" In retrospect, I think that most of those professionals must have known he had autism, but either they were not in a position to offer an opinion, or they did not want to be the bearer of bad news. As the frequency of Richard's blank stares increased, however, I started asking people directly, "Do you think he has autism?" This was in 1991, when few professionals were familiar with the symptoms of the higher functioning forms of autism. Most assured me that Richard was simply "too social" to be autistic and, even worse, a child psychologist suggested that there was "nothing wrong with Richard that a little more 'stimulation' wouldn't correct."

Mortified at the suggestion that I hadn't properly stimulated my son, I asked Richard's preschool teacher if she thought that was the case. She assured me that I was a very good mother and asked me if I had taken Richard to see a neurologist. A neurologist? No, I hadn't, but I was thrilled by the suggestion. Finally someone had offered something helpful! Not even Richard's pediatrician had suggested any type of follow-up with a specialist, even though she knew I was desperately seeking answers. Driving home with the suggestion of calling a neurologist still ringing in my ears, I was both excited and furious that no one had made the suggestion previously. I didn't appreciate the fact that professionals had withheld what seemed like such a "no-brainer" suggestion from me, especially knowing that I myself had suspected autism.

I Could See a Light at the End of the Tunnel, but Why Was the Tunnel so @#*! Long?

Excited to finally have a useful lead, I called to make an appointment with our local pediatric neurologist, only to hear I would have to wait three months for the appointment. The wait was excruciating. It occurred to me that once we finally saw the doctor, there would probably be several tests before we were given a diagnosis. Wrong. Within ten minutes of observing my son's behavior in her office, the doctor looked at me incredulously and asked, "Don't you know what this is? Look at him! He has autism!" (This particular physician is not known for her bedside manner.)

Whoa—that hit me like a ton of bricks! Sure, I had wanted to know—and, as I said, I had even suspected autism myself. But after having countless professionals dismiss my concerns, the abruptness of the diagnosis took me by surprise. To make it even worse, I was alone there with my two children. I was so certain that this appointment would simply be a preliminary intake that I told Richard's father that he didn't need to come with me, that I would probably need him more later. So, there I was on the way home, just me, a three-year-old with autism, his six-month-old sister, and the worst news of my life ringing in my brain. Teary-eyed, I looked back at the children and realized they were asleep. At the very first opportunity, I pulled the car off the road and sat there, sobbing hysterically, thankful for their timely slumber. (You will note that I spent a lot of time crying in my car.)

Richard went through all of the typical tests—Blood, urine, magnetic resonance imaging (MRI), electroencephalogram (EEG), and more—to rule out possible biological causes for his autistic-like behavior.

It took six months to get all of the results, which finally confirmed the autism diagnosis. On that day, I stepped solidly into the realm of acceptance. This, after all the guessing and worry, was something of a relief. My relief, however, was soon joined by a profound sense of loss.

The "Cycle Of Grief" Is Much like a Unicycle—You Feel Alone *and* Off-Balance!

During my many journeys through denial to acceptance and back again, I have become intimately familiar with the "cycle of grief."

Cycle of Grief
(typical pattern)

Please note that the diagram is a sample of a typical cycle. No two people's cycles will ever be alike, and any given individual's cycle may change from crisis to crisis. During the period following Richards diagnosis, I jumped out of denial straight into a combination of shock and anger, followed closely by isolation, depression, and guilt. I have experienced all of the feelings listed on the diagram, many times, and in many combinations.

Learning that your child has special needs creates a tremendous sense of loss, and parents have various ways of coping with this kind of grief. You and your spouse will likely wrack your brains trying to figure out what caused the autism. Each of you may blame yourselves, or worse, each other.

My first instinct was to blame myself—was it that glass of wine I drank during the first trimester, or those "social drugs" I experimented with in my early twenties? As I got more sophisticated in my self-blame, I thought it must have been something karmic, perhaps a punishment for some error or wrong-doing just prior to my pregnancy. As I read more about autism and its actual causes, I started to question the following possibilities:

- The poorly-ventilated office where I worked during the early part of my pregnancy had been sprayed by an exterminator. Exposure to insecticides has been proven to cause autism.

- My mother had worked at an optical products factory during much of my childhood. I learned that there were hundreds of families with autistic children in Massachusetts who either lived near, or whose family members had worked at, another major optical factory. I assumed that similar, potentially damaging chemicals were used at both plants.

- The many vaccinations Richard had been given, especially those from birth-18 months.

Richard's father blamed the fertility drug I had taken. He held fast to that assumption for years, although there was little or no research to prove his theory. We were both angry and needed to blame something or someone. What it all boils down to, however, is that there is absolutely no way of ever knowing for sure what caused the autism—although I still can't help but wonder.

Our Own Circle of Sadness

Riddled with sadness and self-imposed guilt, I sat and cried for about a month as Richard's father searched for statistics (the incidence of autism, what level of functioning Richard had achieved, what we could expect, etc.). Later, as I came out of my funk, I starting reading every book on autism that I could find, and later founded an autism support group. Richard's father dove into his work and pretty much stayed there, as if somehow things would be okay if only he could earn enough money. We both developed a strong sense of purpose and duty but, more often than not, could not be there for each other emotionally.

In counseling during the breakup of my marriage to Richard's father, my therapist (who specializes in working with autistic children) said, "The moment a child is diagnosed, it should be *mandatory* that the parents seek counseling immediately and stay in counseling for years. Coping with something like autism is just too difficult for most couples to handle on their own!" While I can honestly say that Richard's autism was not the cause of my divorce, it did facilitate a further breakdown in communication as we each tried to cope with the situation as best we could.

Extended family members are also likely to grieve when you tell them of your child's challenges. Their methods of grieving, however, may baffle you. Some family members will be incredibly understanding and helpful, while others may become distant, or perhaps even find a way to blame *you*. Grandparents, aunts, and uncles, firmly in denial, will often assert that the child's behaviors are a result of bad parenting, or that you are making a "mountain out of a molehill." The news seems to hit some grandparents particularly hard. Many will try to remain in denial mode, and will have to struggle twice upon acceptance: they will grieve for the loss of their beloved grandchild's (presumed) full potential, and they will grieve for their own children and the challenges they are facing. I was very fortunate to have, for the most part, loving and accepting family and friends around me through our many trials.

Learning that your child has autism will also test some of your friendships. Many of your friends will try to be in denial for you. They may look at some of your child's eccentricities and try to relate them to some of you and your spouse's traits. Some well-meaning friends will insist they know what is best and will try to tell you how to "handle" the situation. Following my son's diagnosis I remember talking to one of my friends about his special education program. She was incredulous. "Don't let them label your child!" she insisted. "He will never live it down and you'll regret it." That didn't make any sense to me. My child actually did have autism, so why should I be afraid to allow the education system to label him as such? Wasn't that his best shot for getting the care and education he needed? Even though I felt good about my choices on Richard's behalf, deep-down this kind of adamant suggestion really threw me off—forcing me to constantly second-guess myself and spend more time that I would have liked in "Guilt-ville."

As you will learn over time, your true friends will stand by you. At first they may offer up some denial for you (that's a friend's job after all!), but you will eventually grow to count on them for much-needed acceptance and support. They will be the first to lend a shoulder to cry on, to baby-sit your "challenging youngster" (even though deep-down they are probably scared to death the child will freak out on them), and to listen to you go on and on (ad nausem) about autism. Be careful, though, not to burn out these good-hearted souls. There is a limit to every friendship; there must be a balance of give and take.

If at all possible, make friends with other parents of children with autism. I have my "autism friends," and friends whose children are more "typical." I have learned to balance the friends in my life, leaning heavily on my autism friends for unconditional understanding, and on other friends for an escape from autism's constant presence.

In discussing friendships with my support group members, many are saddened by the loss of some of their former best friends following the diagnosis of their child. I used to feel the same way until it occurred to me that friendships tend to be cyclical. We lose many of our "best friends" the second we leave for college, many more when we get married, and more still when we have a baby. Our friends change as a matter of course as our lives change. Somehow, though, it seems more hurtful to have a friend seemingly desert you because your child has a disability. Then, it becomes intentional and highly personal!

Shop, Drop, and Roll!

Even more difficult than the disappointment over losing friends was the constant worry about what people were thinking about Richard's antics—and my skills (or lack thereof) as a parent. Going out in public with Richard was, simply put, a trial. No matter where we went, whether it was the grocery store, the post office, or the library, he would make a scene. His favorite was to drop down on the floor and either lay flat on his face, spread-eagled, or to roll. He "spit polished" many a department store floor! The shinier the flooring, the more he loved to slide or roll along them. Any attempt at getting him to stand up would result in a blood-curdling scream.

People would look at us, wondering why I would put up with such behavior. One day at our local post office, an older woman (who clearly had been weaned on a persimmon) tapped Richard sternly on the shoulder and insisted "You need to learn to behave, young man!" Generally when this happens I treat it as a teaching opportunity, and inform the offender that Richard has autism and he is doing the best he can to cope under that particular social situation. This usually works like a charm, diffusing hasty judgments and furthering the cause of autism awareness. In this case, however, I was so shocked by this woman's harshness that I scooped Richard up silently and took him out to the car. This time I couldn't even wait until Richard had fallen asleep—the tears were uncontrollable.

Taking the kids out of the house became an increasingly difficult chore, complicated further by the huge chip I was carrying on my shoulder. Paranoia set in; I assumed that literally everyone was judging us, everywhere we went. One day, though, a stranger validated me in a way that changed my attitude forever. The kids and I were in a fabric store in our local mall. Laura was about nine months old and I was pushing her in a stroller. Richard was about three at the time, and was content to spin himself around in circles as we waited in a seemingly endless line. After about fifteen minutes of waiting, baby Laura had had enough and started screaming. I didn't want to leave the line because I had already waited so long; I was next, so as Laura screamed, I waited. Finally, I paid for my fabric and we left the store.

As we walked out into the center aisle of the mall, I sensed that we were being followed. I turned quickly and saw a man looking right at us. "Oh man," I thought, "here we go again. I wonder what obnoxious opinion *he* has about how I am raising my children." I didn't look back again, but started heading out the door into the parking lot. My heart started pounding as he followed us out the door. "Excuse me, Miss," he said. I turned, and with a defensive air offered, "Yes?"

"All I can say is *good for you*!" he said, with a determined smile.

"What?" I asked, caught totally off guard by the compliment.

"Back there, when your daughter started screaming—you just let her cry. Good for you! My daughters are spoiling their kids rotten—the second they cry, they get picked up and coddled. Brats, the lot of them!"

I thanked the man for his thoughts, and breathed a heavy sigh of relief as I secured the kids in their car seats. On that day, for the first time in a long time, I felt competent as a parent and I was able to get behind the wheel of my car *without crying*!

To Cope, or Not to Cope—That Is *Not* an Option

During one of my support group meetings years ago I was speaking about autism's emotional toll on parents. During this talk, I admitted freely that I was taking an antidepressant, and had been for well over a year. I encouraged parents to maintain their mental health and to "shamelessly" seek counseling and "take the drugs" if they felt they were needed. During the discussions that followed, over three-fourths of the members in the room admitted that they were also taking anti-depressants and anti-anxiety medications. As the meeting broke up, several other members pulled me aside and thanked me for my honesty, admitting that they recently had begun taking medication and that they were ashamed to admit it to anyone. One in particular said that she "felt so much better about taking the medications, knowing that she was not alone, and that she was not nuts." I replied "Well, nuts is relative." We laughed and she gave me a big hug of thanks.

Grandpa May Have Walked Four Miles a Day (in the Snow) to School, but Nothing Compares with Putting Your Three-Year-Old on a Bus!

In preparing for Richard's placement into a public special needs preschool, I was first introduced to the Individualized Education Plan (IEP). I recall Richard's preschool teacher looking at the IEP proposed by the folks at the early intervention center and commenting, "This is the *longest* IEP we have ever seen!" I soothed myself by thinking, "Wow, they must really care about him to have written such a comprehensive plan!" Denial really does have its merits—it allowed me to leave this meeting feeling quite good, instead of overwhelmed by the reality of the long road ahead. So, on the first day of school I found the courage to put my tiny little boy on that special needs bus, said a prayer for him, and spent the morning back in bed—crying.

That was in 1990. There have since been many IEPs (all of them long ones), many different bus drivers, and many mornings with me back in bed.

Laura and Richard — Playing in Great Grandma's Tub!

I am thankful to have two great kids who, more often than not, have been my strength through our most difficult moments. Naturally, I worry about them too. Richard receives a great deal of attention (good and bad) and I am often concerned that Laura will feel left out, eventually coming to resent Richard. One day I asked Laura how she felt about having a brother with autism and she was surprisingly positive. She was clearly proud of Richard and his kind-hearted nature. Her main concerns were for his safety, particularly with fire and stranger dangers. She did, however, confess that she was glad Richard didn't run around naked in front of her friends anymore!

Richard and his "Step-Daddy"

Richard, Laura, and I have traveled over many bumpy roads together. We are happy to have reached such a happy place with Sibley in our lives (we were married in 1990). In taking stock of how these experiences have affected me personally, it occurs to me that I have:

- Gained a lot of weight (emotional eating).
- Sought counseling, taken antidepressants.
- Never gotten enough sleep.
- Gotten divorced.
- Supported the tissue industry!

But, in those nine years, I have also grown immensely as a person, having learned a great deal about:

- Autism and its many facets.
- Special education and my important role as a parent.
- Family dynamics and the importance of communication.
- The rights of people with special needs.
- Tolerance.
- My own emotional strength.
- Late night television (during times when Richard wasn't sleeping).
- True friendship, through thick and thin.
- Conditional and unconditional love.

Reflections of a Bumpy Road

Think about back roads you may have traveled in your life. Perhaps you were going a bit too fast and hit a sudden dip. At first, you panicked as you felt the world drop out from under you, your stomach in your throat. Then you probably experienced a feeling of exhilaration, your body tingling as it readjusted. If you are anything like me, the next time you went over that same hill you sped up a bit—the fear gave way to thrilling anticipation!

The reality of autism is much like that uncertain ride on a back road. There are bumps, twists, detours, washouts, and some shocking dips. I can't say that it is ever easy; however, with each subsequent ride down Autism Road, I find myself becoming more confident and better able to anticipate and avoid potential problems. I am even beginning to appreciate certain aspects of the adventure.

Supporting and Accepting Richard's Right to Take His Own Path

Over the years I have been privileged to meet many adults with autism who have shared their stories with me, either through casual conversation or as conference presenters. Each time I meet one of these extraordinary individuals I walk away with the belief that not only will Richard be "okay" as he grows older, but he can have a quality life. I also have learned that things like driving or getting married are not nearly as important as him feeling good about himself, being able to make many of his own choices, and finding meaningful employment.

I have gained another very important perspective from the adults with autism whom I have met; specifically, that Richard is not "broken" because of his autism, and does not necessarily need to be "fixed" by me or anyone else. The autism is a large part of who he is and, given a choice, it is likely that he would not wish to have his autistic side taken away. Without exception, the autistic adults simply want to be supported and accepted for who they are—resenting the notion that society considers them deficient or diseased.

A large part of accepting Richard and helping him achieve a high quality of life is to include him in our lives as often as possible. When Sibley and I were married, my daughter Laura was my maid of honor, and Richard was

Sibley's best man. Just prior to the ceremony, I said to Sibley, "Don't worry; I won't be upset if everything doesn't go perfectly." Richard had struggled through the rehearsals and had ultimately decided to sit with the guests rather than stand with the wedding party. In the middle of the ceremony, however, Richard walked up between Sibley and me, wrapped his arms around our shoulders, and said our vows with us! At first, we were tempted to quiet him, but we quickly realized his actions provided us with a once-in-a-lifetime moment—one that only Richard could have made possible.

Whether Richard is making an older woman's day by loudly asserting, "I think you're beautiful!" or scaring me when he turns around and hugs a total stranger, the fact is that Richard deserves to be accepted for who he is and he has the right to experience his life in his own unique way. We will continue to encourage Richard to live his life to its fullest, while teaching him enough about potential dangers to keep him out of harm's way. I am thankful that Richard is only 14. We still have a great deal to teach him—and vice-versa.

About the Authors

Abby & Sibley Collins are the founders of Phat Art 4 Publishing and co-authors of the on-line course *A Family's Journey into Autism*. They are also the proud parents of Kimberly, Stephany, Richard (14-year old son with autism) and Laura. Details of their autism experience follows:

Abby Ward Collins is the former Executive Director and founder of Potential Unlimited Publishing and the Autism Support & Advocacy Project, and is the author of the children's book, *Captain Tommy*. Abby is a nationally-known speaker with topics including: *Proactive Peer Tutoring*; *The Rules Do Not Apply: Disregarding Much of What You Know in Order to Creatively Care for a Child with Autism;* and *Autism & Adolescence: The Middle Years*. Abby's parent perspective and sense of humor leave a memorable impression on her audiences.

Sibley J. Collins retired from the Air Force in 1992 after 20 years of service. Following his Air Force career, Sibley earned his AA in General Studies, his BAS in Human Services and became a Certified Hypnotherapist in 1999. Sibley has worked as a case manager for children with behavior problems and for developmentally disabled adults. Sibley is a frequent workshop presenter, sharing his perspective as a stepfather and case manager. Sibley has conducted social skills/life skills classes for children and adults with developmental disabilities.

About the Illustrator

Kimberly Owsley is Phat Art 4's Midwest Regional Manager. In that capacity, Kim facilitates Phat Art 4's autism conferences, bookstore events and distribution in the Midwest. Prior to joining Phat Art 4, Kim had over 10 years of experience in the printing industry. Her hobbies include art, cooking, and collecting antiques. Kim and her husband, Matt, live in Missouri.

About Phat Art 4

Phat Art 4 is a company dedicated to publishing and distributing down-to-earth books on autism, Asperger Syndrome and related disorders. Phat Art 4 also provides quality bookstores at autism-related conferences and workshops nationwide.

The Story Behind Our Name

Prior to launching Phat Art 4 in November 2000, founders Sibley & Abby Collins began offering social skills groups to children with developmental disabilities. They wanted the groups to have a name the children could relate to, so they thought about positive slang terms used by today's kids. The word "Phat," which means "cool" or "well-built," was chosen and then Sibley suggested "Phat Art" because of their desire at that time to also offer art and drama enrichment.

Much to Sibley's surprise, Abby became a bit emotional at the suggestion. What Sibley didn't know was that "Fat Art" was the nickname of her long-deceased father!

The "4" was added at the suggestion of a psychic-friend of Abby's. According to the principals of numerology, the combination of Phat + Art + 4 adds up to "fame & fortune."

Who could argue with that???

How to Order Additional Copies

AUTISM: Now What? can be purchased directly from the publisher:

Phat Art 4
P.O. Box 711
Stratham, NH 03885-0711
Telephone: 603-778-9990
Toll-Free: 866-742-8278
www.phatart4.com

Retail Price: $9.95

Quantity discounts available to autism societies, support groups, non-profit agencies and book distributors. Please call for discount rate information.

Visa, MasterCard, American Express, Personal Checks & Purchase Orders accepted.

✍ ✍

Phat Art 4 offers over 150 books on autism, Asperger Syndrome and related disorders. Please visit our website or call toll-free to request a catalog.

FREE SHIPPING & HANDLING